Thinking about Interest Rates, Prices, and the Economy

Instructors' Guide to

Interest Rates, Prices, and the Economy

Jerry Mushin

Victoria University of Wellington,
New Zealand

SCIENTIFIC PUBLISHERS (INDIA)

P.O. BOX 91 JODHPUR (RAJ.)

Published by:
Tanay Sharma
Scientific Publishers (India)
5-A, New Pali Road, P.O. Box 91
Jodhpur - 342 001 (India)

Tel.: +91-291-2433323
Fax: + 91-291-2613449

E-mail: info@scientificpub.com
www.scientificpub.com

ISBN: 978-81-7233-577-9

Lasertype set: Rajesh Ojha
Printed in India

Acknowledgements

My greatest debt is to my students, especially those who have asked incisive questions and expected lucid answers. I also thank my colleagues, and my wife Claudia and our son Stephen, for their continued interest and encouragement.

Contents

Introduction

Interest Rates, Prices, and the Economy (Scientific Publishers (India), Jodhpur, 2009) is principally intended to be a textbook for introductory undergraduate courses in macroeconomic theory. The purpose of *Thinking about Interest Rates, Prices, and the Economy* is to assist instructors, particularly those who are inexperienced, to identify the key objectives, and the parts that students are likely to find confusing, of each chapter of this textbook.

Although it includes no advanced mathematics, *Interest Rates, Prices, and the Economy* introduces students to the nature of macroeconomic models. Graphs and simple algebra are used extensively. The aim is that, in addition to acquiring rigorous knowledge of the model that is presented in this book, students will become familiar with the nature of economic models in general. This will give them skills that will be of value when undertaking more advanced courses in economics and in other subjects.

Applied Material

Although *Interest Rates, Prices, and the Economy* is a textbook of theory, Chapters 1, 4, 9, 10, and 11 include a significant amount of applied material. This is intended to show the relevance of the theoretical content. It should also be of interest in its own right. Ultimately, theory has value only if it increases understanding of the real world.

To enhance their understanding of macroeconomic theory, and to increase their interest in the subject, students should be encouraged (or required) to assemble recent data and use their knowledge of theory to comment. The principal sources of recent Indian macroeconomic data are listed in the Further Reading appendix of

Interest Rates, Prices, and the Economy. Data on real GDP and nominal GDP (and their components), the money supply, interest rates, unemployment, the price level, and exchange rates are especially useful. Other relevant variables include the government budget balance and the international trade balance. Students should also be encouraged to use their knowledge of theory to comment on current news items that are of macroeconomic interest.

The applied content of *Interest Rates, Prices, and the Economy* refers to the Indian economy. It is useful to compare the recent macroeconomic experience, and the data definitions, of other countries. There are many sources of international data. If the United States or New Zealand are the countries with which comparisons are made, the easiest way to find the relevant information is to refer to the books on which *Interest Rates, Prices, and the Economy* is based:

Jerry Mushin: *Output and the Role of Money*, World Scientific Publishing Company, New York, London, and Singapore, 2002.

Jerry Mushin: *Income, Interest Rates and Prices* [3rd ed], The Dunmore Press Ltd, Palmerston North, New Zealand, 1999.

Chapter 4 of *Interest Rates, Prices, and the Economy* includes a brief description of the monetary policy instruments that are used by the Reserve Bank of India [www.rbi.gov.in], from whom more details can be obtained. Additional information on monetary policy in the United States is available from the Federal Reserve System [www.federalreserve.gov]. Additional information on monetary policy in New Zealand is available from the Reserve Bank of New Zealand [www.rbnz.govt.nz].

An important resource related to Chapter 11 of *Interest Rates, Prices, and the Economy* is:

International Financial Statistics, International Monetary Fund, Washington, DC.

Each issue of this monthly publication contains, in addition to a wide range of macroeconomic data, information on the exchange-rate régime of each country and territory that is an IMF member. Floating (or managed floating) exchange rate systems predominate (although some countries that claim to have managed floating exchange rates are actually stabilizing the value of their currencies with respect to the United States dollar or some other major currency). Information is also available directly from the International Monetary Fund [www.imf.org].

Multiple-Choice Questions

The multiple-choice questions in *Thinking about Interest Rates, Prices, and the Economy* have been used many times. The list of questions is intended to be indicative and not prescriptive. The questions can be adapted to refer to local conditions and to the interests of students. They are intended to be a resource for the use of instructors and not a complete assessment scheme.

The questions are not of equal difficulty. Although some of the questions merely test knowledge of a definition, many will require considerable thought. It is, of course, important that questions are challenging. Students do not learn from, and feel cheated by, questions that are too easy. Learning to manipulate an economic model increases understanding both of that model and of economic models in general.

There is substantial duplication of content in the questions. Approaching each theoretical point in several ways enables students' knowledge to be tested thoroughly. Similarly, the calculations are not intended to test mathematical skills. Although mathematical callisthenics might be of value, calculations are used in *Thinking about Interest Rates, Prices, and the Economy* in order to increase understanding of the relationships between key macroeconomic variables. Multiple-choice questions enable students and their teachers to identify points of difficulty and of confusion.

Macroeconomic theory is a sequential subject, and the content of each chapter of *Interest Rates, Prices, and the Economy* builds on the content of earlier chapters. For this reason, it was frequently not a simple matter to allocate each of the multiple-choice questions in *Thinking about Interest Rates, Prices, and the Economy* to a particular chapter. The rule that has been applied is that each question under a particular chapter heading can be attempted without reading the later chapters. Chapters are neither of equal length nor of equal importance, and the number of questions under each chapter heading varies substantially.

Previous Study of Microeconomics

It would be advantageous if students had already completed a basic course in microeconomics before beginning their study of macroeconomics. Although elasticity of demand is the only theoretical device in microeconomics that is used in *Interest Rates, Prices, and the Economy*, it would be helpful if students were already familiar with the nature of economic models, with the concept of an equilibrium, and with the meaning of *ceteris paribus*. The multiple-choice questions in this introductory section of *Thinking about Interest Rates, Prices, and the Economy* are intended to test students' knowledge of the essential basic concepts that are needed before reading *Interest Rates, Prices, and the Economy*.

0.1 The meaning of *ceteris paribus* (other things being equal) is:

(a) accurate economic predictions are possible (even if improbable)

(b) the theory ignores errors in economic data

(c) the theory assumes no change in variables that are not explicitly mentioned

(d) the government does not attempt to solve economic problems

0.2 The *ceteris paribus* assumption means that:

(a) variables not explicitly mentioned are constant

(b) the government does not interfere with economic decisions

(c) prices move quickly to their equilibrium levels

(d) prices move slowly to their equilibrium levels

0.3 In economic models, the equilibrium outcome is:

(a) generally regarded as socially desirable

(b) likely to be induced by decreased taxation

(c) the point towards which the system moves immediately

(d) the point towards which the system moves eventually

0.4 An economic model is a simplified description of:

(a) the political opinions of the author

(b) at least one economic policy objective of the government

(c) observed behaviour

(d) behaviour that is morally right

0.5 A 1.99% increase in the price of a commodity whose elasticity of demand has an absolute value of 1.99 causes a decrease in the quantity demanded of:

(a) greater than 1.99% and an increase in sales revenue

(b) greater than 1.99% and a decrease in sales revenue

(c) less than 1.99% and an increase in sales revenue

(d) less than 1.99% and a decrease in sales revenue

0.6 When the absolute value of the elasticity of demand of a particular commodity is greater than one, an increase in its price leads to:

(a) an increase in sales revenue

(b) a decrease in sales revenue

(c) no change in sales revenue

(d) (a) or (b) or (c)

0.7 In an economic model, the equilibrium is the position that:

(a) is imposed by the government

(b) the government wishes the economy to reach

(c) the system moves towards spontaneously

(d) always occurs

1

The Nature of Macroeconomic Issues

This chapter begins with a discussion of the nature of macroeconomics, which differs in important ways from microeconomics. The key issues include data problems and aggregation problems. Also important is the nature of a macroeconomic equilibrium, and particularly that the achievement of a stable value of an aggregate economic variable probably does not mean that a general equilibrium has been reached. A total can be stable while its components are changing.

The extent of disagreement among its practitioners is also one of the distinguishing features of macroeconomics. In many cases, there is no clear resolution to disagreement between schools of thought. The main points of difference between the theoretical approaches explained in *Interest Rates, Prices, and the Economy* are summarised in Chapter 14.

National accounts data are discussed partly as an example of a measurement problem in macroeconomics. It is important to emphasise the weaknesses of these data. One of these is that errors in the data might compound other errors to create errors that are even more serious. The precise meanings of the technical words that are used in Table 1 are important especially since several, including consumption, investment, and income, have meanings in macroeconomics that differ from their meanings in conversational use.

1.1 In the calculation of Gross Domestic Product, the value of imports is subtracted from the total because:

(a) other countries have lower wage rates and can produce goods more cheaply

(b) some countries forbid imports

(c) many people do not know whether they are buying imports

(d) other categories of expenditure include imports

1.2 National Income is:

(a) the revenue received by selling goods and services in other countries

(b) a measure of the value of aggregate output

(c) the total of all persons' incomes plus social security payments etc.

(d) the amount received in net taxation by the government

1.3 The difference between Gross Domestic Product and Gross National Product is the:

(a) net indirect tax revenue

(b) balance of trade surplus or deficit

(c) government budget surplus or deficit

(d) net foreign factor income

1.4 In order to calculate Net National Product, depreciation is subtracted from Gross National Product:

(a) as a proxy for capital consumption

(b) because the population is

(c) because an increasing proportion of the population is in the labour force

(d) because most investment expenditure is financed with borrowed money

1.5 The level of investment expenditure is of particular interest to macro-economists because it:

(a) does not vary much from one year to the next

(b) is probably less than the value of exports

(c) is a major influence on the rate of economic growth

(d) leads to immediate increases in profits

1.6 The calculation of real GDP from nominal GDP allows for:

(a) subsidies and indirect taxes

(b) changes in the government budget deficit

(c) changes in the price level

(d) capital consumption

1.7 The calculation of Net National Product from Gross National Product allows for:

(a) subsidies and indirect taxes

(b) changes in the government budget deficit

(c) changes in the price level

(d) capital consumption

1.8 The purchase by a company of a machine is not included in fixed investment data unless:

(a) it is new (not second-hand)

(b) the company intends to own it for at least three years

(c) (a) and (b)

(d) neither (a) nor (b)

2

Determinants and Significance of Aggregate Demand

This chapter contains an introduction to the Keynesian model of aggregate income determination. The key point is that changes in income cause changes in aggregate demand (through the functional relationships of some of its components) and *vice versa* (through the multiplier process). It is essential that students understand the categories of aggregate demand [$E_P \equiv C + I + G + (X - Z)$] and the relationships of each of these with the level of income and with other independent variables. The nature of fiscal policy and the meaning of full employment are also explained.

In this chapter, the levels of interest rates, prices, the money supply, and exchange rates are assumed to be constant.

This chapter is also an introduction to economic model building. It draws attention to the nature of an equilibrium, to the distinction between a definition and a behavioural relationship, to the distinction between a dependent variable and an independent variable, to the distinction between a variable and a parameter, and to the distinction between the *ex-ante* and *ex-post* values of certain variables.

2.1 Consumption expenditure is:

(a) entirely autonomous

(b) partly autonomous

(c) fixed

(d) specified by the government

2.2 Investment expenditure is:

(a) entirely autonomous

(b) partly autonomous
(c) fixed
(d) specified by the government

2.3 Expenditure on exports is:
(a) entirely autonomous
(b) partly autonomous
(c) fixed
(d) specified by the government

2.4 Expenditure on imports is:
(a) entirely autonomous
(b) partly autonomous
(c) fixed
(d) specified by the government

2.5 An increase in investment expenditure:
(a) might be caused by an improvement in confidence
(b) might cause an improvement in confidence
(c) (a) and (b)
(d) neither (a) nor (b)

2.6 An increase in consumption expenditure:
(a) might be caused by an improvement in confidence
(b) might cause an improvement in confidence
(c) (a) and (b)
(d) neither (a) nor (b)

2.7 When income increases:
(a) consumption expenditure increases
(b) investment expenditure decreases
(c) exports increase
(d) imports decrease

2.8 The consumption function (graphed against disposable income [Y_d]) shifts if there is a change in:
(a) income

(b) confidence
(c) net taxation
(d) government expenditure on goods and services

2.9 An increase in income causes:

(a) a decrease in imports
(b) a decrease in imports and an increase in exports
(c) an increase in imports
(d) an increase in imports and a decrease in exports

2.10 Savings refers to:

(a) the part of income that is not spent
(b) the part of income that is not earned
(c) accumulation of money
(d) accumulation of money and purchases of financial assets

2.11 The circular flow of income model shows that:

(a) decisions in any part of the economy affect every other part of the economy
(b) firms do not care about the welfare of their employees
(c) there are neither taxes nor subsidies
(d) firms do not trade with other firms

2.12 The planned expenditure line [E_P] shifts upward if:

(a) government expenditure increases
(b) marginal propensity to consume increases
(c) marginal propensity to tax increases
(d) (a) and (b)

2.13 The planned expenditure line [E_P] shifts clockwise if:

(a) government expenditure increases
(b) marginal propensity to consume increases
(c) marginal propensity to tax increases
(d) (b) and (c)

2.14 If the behavioural equation for net tax revenue is $T = -25 + 0.35Y$:

(a) autonomous net taxation is greater than induced net taxation

(b) there is a budget surplus if income is equal to 120

(c) there is a budget deficit if income is equal to 120

(d) neither (a) nor (b) nor (c)

2.15 The marginal propensity to consume [b] is constant with respect to changes in disposable income [Y_d] if:

(a) autonomous consumption [a] is positive

(b) the consumption function is linear

(c) disposable income is equally distributed among the population

(d) the value of the marginal propensity to tax [t] is less than one

2.16 If the government budget is in balance:

(a) income is at the full-employment level

(b) income is at the equilibrium level

(c) net taxation is equal to government spending on goods and services

(d) net foreign factor income is zero

2.17 Expenditure on exports from India depends on:

(a) income in India

(b) income in other countries

(c) (a) and (b)

(d) neither (a) nor (b)

2.18 In the short term, an increase in aggregate income:

(a) increases aggregate demand by a smaller amount

(b) increases aggregate demand by the same amount

(c) increases aggregate demand by a larger amount

(d) has no effect on aggregate demand

2.19 In the long term, assuming that there are no effects on prices and interest rates, a decrease in aggregate expenditure:

(a) decreases aggregate income by a smaller amount

(b) decreases aggregate income by the same amount

(c) decreases aggregate income by a larger amount

(d) has no effect on aggregate income

2.20 A stable level of output occurs when:

(a) the government budget balance is zero

(b) *ex-ante* injections [J] is equal to withdrawals [W]

(c) *ex-post* injections is equal to withdrawals

(d) (a) and (c)

2.21 If the government increases its expenditure on goods and services by Rs. 2 crore per year, assuming that there are no effects on prices and interest rates, aggregate income increases by:

(a) about Rs. 2 crore per year

(b) significantly more than Rs. 2 crore per year

(c) slightly more than Rs. 2 crore per year

(d) slightly less than Rs. 2 crore per year

2.22 Following a disturbance, the new equilibrium level of income is:

(a) not always socially optimum

(b) likely to be reached immediately

(c) an objective of the government

(d) likely to return to its original level in the long term

2.23 The value of the income-expenditure multiplier [K] depends on the:

(a) amount of government spending on goods and services

(b) response to a change of income

(c) level of autonomous expenditure

(d) size of the government budget deficit

2.24 The aggregate expenditure function [E_P] shifts if:

(a) there is an increase in consumption spending following a change in net tax rates

(b) there is an autonomous increase in consumption spending

(c) firms decrease production following an unplanned increase in the level of stocks

(d) (a) and (b)

2.25 Aggregate income [Y] is at its equilibrium level when it is equal to:

(a) *ex-ante* expenditure

(b) *ex-post* expenditure

(c) the difference between *ex-ante* expenditure and *ex-post* expenditure

(d) the sum of *ex-ante* expenditure and *ex-post* expenditure

2.26 The possible causes of an increase in the value of the income-expenditure multiplier [K] include an increase in:

(a) autonomous consumption expenditure

(b) the marginal propensity to import

(c) the marginal propensity to consume

(d) expenditure on exports

2.27 Following an increase in the value of the income-expenditure multiplier, [K] an increase in government spending on goods and services:

(a) increases equilibrium income by a greater amount than previously

(b) increases autonomous consumption expenditure

(c) decreases the marginal propensity to import

(d) increases the marginal propensity to import

2.28 The income-expenditure multiplier [K] shows:

(a) the effect on income [Y] of an autonomous change in expenditure [E_P]

(b) the effect on expenditure of an autonomous change in income

(c) the proportion of a change in disposable income [Y_d] that is not spent

(d) the proportion of a change in income [Y] that is not spent

2.29 The income-expenditure multiplier [K] increases if:

(a) the marginal propensity to import decreases

(b) the marginal propensity to consume decreases

(c) government expenditure is decreased when the government budget is in surplus

(d) government expenditure is decreased when the government budget is in deficit

2.30 Unplanned investment in stocks occurs when:

(a) planned expenditure is greater than income

(b) planned expenditure is less than income

(c) planned expenditure is equal to income

(d) (b) and (c)

2.31 When income is at its equilibrium level:

(a) every firm has a stable level of output

(b) firms' increases in output cancel with other firms' decreases in output

(c) there is no unemployment

(d) there is neither unemployment nor inflation

2.32 The intersection of a planned expenditure line [E_P] and a 45° line is the point where:

(a) *ex-post* expenditure is equal to income

(b) *ex-ante* expenditure is equal to income

(c) *ex-ante* expenditure is equal to *ex-post* expenditure

(d) (a) and (b) and (c)

2.33 Full employment:

(a) occurs if the economy is at the equilibrium level of output

(b) never occurs spontaneously

(c) occurs if all companies are technically efficient

(d) neither (a) nor (b) nor (c)

2.34 Tight fiscal policy shifts the:

(a) injections line downward

(b) injections line downward or shifts the withdrawals line upward

(c) withdrawals line downward and shifts the injections line upward

(d) withdrawals line upward and/or shifts the injections line downward

2.35 When income is at the full-employment level:

(a) everyone is working

(b) everyone is working full time (not part time)

(c) the level of wage rates is stable

(d) neither (a) nor (b) nor (c)

2.36 Fiscal policy means changes in net tax rates and/or in government spending that are designed to:

(a) decrease unemployment

(b) decrease the rate of inflation

(c) increase the rate of inflation

(d) affect the level of aggregate demand

2.37 If the level of income [Y] has a weak influence on the level of imports [Z], the planned expenditure line [E_P] is:

(a) horizontal

(b) vertical

(c) steep

(d) not steep

2.38 If the level of income [Y] has a weak influence on the level of net taxation [T], the planned expenditure line [E_P] is:

(a) horizontal

(b) vertical

(c) steep

(d) not steep

2.39 Identify the decision that necessarily tightens fiscal policy:

(a) an increase in government expenditure and a decrease in net taxation

(b) an increase in government expenditure and an increase in net taxation

(c) a decrease in government expenditure and a decrease in net taxation

(d) a decrease in government expenditure and an increase in net taxation

2.40 Tight fiscal policy causes:

(a) a downward shift of the withdrawals function and/or an upward shift of the injections function

(b) a downward shift of the withdrawals function and/or a downward shift of the injections function

(c) an upward shift of the withdrawals function and/or an upward shift of the injections function

(d) an upward shift of the withdrawals function and/or a downward shift of the injections function

2.41 A government that uses fiscal policy to decrease unemployment is attempting to:

(a) move the equilibrium level of income towards the full-employment level of income

(b) move the full-employment level of income towards the equilibrium level of income

(c) increase the level of income to a point where it is above the equilibrium level of income and equal to or below the full-employment level of income

(d) neither (a) nor (b) nor (c)

2.42 In the consumption function:

$$C = a + bY_d$$

the independent variable(s) is/are:

(a) a

(b) a and b

(c) Y_d

(d) Y_d and a

2.43 In the consumption function:

$$C = a + bY_d$$

the dependent variable is:

(a) C

(b) a

(c) b

(d) Y_d

2.44 In the consumption function:

$$C = a + bY_d$$

the parameter(s) is/are:

(a) a

(b) b

(c) a and b

(d) a, b, and Y_d

3

The *IS* Line: Income, Interest Rates, and the Goods Market

In this chapter, an additional independent variable, the level of interest rates [r], is introduced into the model. This means that the behavioural equation for planned expenditure [E_P], and hence for equilibrium income [Y_e], now has two independent variables. In this chapter, the money supply, exchange rates and the price level are assumed to be constant.

The *IS* line, the locus of income-equilibrium combinations of Y and of r, is derived. The effects of autonomous disturbances on the *IS* line are analysed.

This chapter also explains the main types of fiscal policy instruments, the balanced budget multiplier theorem, and the indeterminate nature of the relationship between fiscal policy and the size of the government budget deficit or surplus.

3.1 When the level of interest rates [r] increases:

(a) consumption expenditure increases

(b) investment expenditure decreases

(c) exports decrease

(d) the *IS* line shifts to the right

3.2 If the government budget is in deficit, and government spending [G] is decreased, the size of the deficit:

(a) decreases

(b) increases

(c) remains the same

(d) (a) or (b) or (c)

3.3 An increase in the sensitivity of investment [*I*] to changes in income:

(a) makes the *IS* line steeper

(b) makes the *IS* line less steep

(c) shifts the *IS* line to the left

(d) shifts the *IS* line to the right

3.4 An increase in expenditure on exports [*X*]:

(a) shifts the *IS* line to the right

(b) shifts the *IS* line to the left

(c) makes the *IS* line steeper

(d) (a) and (c)

3.5 The *IS* line shows those combinations of income and rate of interest where:

(a) income [*Y*] is stable

(b) the rate of interest [*r*] is stable

(c) (a) and (b)

(d) neither (a) nor (b)

3.6 If there is an increase in government expenditure [*G*], the *IS* line:

(a) shifts to the right

(b) shifts to the left

(c) remains in the same position

(d) (a) or (c)

3.7 Investment expenditure [*I*] is a:

(a) positive function of income and a negative function of the interest rate

(b) positive function of income and a positive function of the interest rate

(c) negative function of income and a negative function of the interest rate

(d) negative function of income and a positive function of the interest rate

3.8 If the investment function shifts

from $I = 324 + 0.12Y - 37r$

to $I = 324 + 0.12Y - 28r$

the *IS* line:

(a) shifts to the left and becomes steeper

(b) shifts to the right and becomes steeper

(c) shifts to the left with no change of gradient

(d) shifts to the right with no change of gradient

3.9 The *IS* locus identifies combinations of income [Y] and rate of interest [r] where income is equal to:

(a) autonomous expenditure

(b) induced expenditure

(c) planned expenditure

(d) planned expenditure [E_P] minus net exports [$X - Z$]

3.10 If there is a government budget surplus and all tax rates are decreased:

(a) income increases and the budget surplus decreases

(b) income increases and the budget surplus might decrease

(c) income decreases and the budget surplus decreases

(d) income decreases and the budget surplus might decrease

3.11 The *IS* line shifts upward if:

(a) government expenditure decreases

(b) the marginal propensity to consume decreases

(c) the marginal propensity to tax decreases

(d) (a) and (b)

3.12 The *IS* line shifts clockwise if:

(a) government expenditure decreases

(b) the marginal propensity to consume decreases

(c) the marginal propensity to tax decreases

(d) (b) and (c)

3.13 An *IS* line is the locus of points where:

(a) income is at the equilibrium level

(b) income is at the full-employment level

(c) the level of interest rates is stable

(d) (a) and (c)

3.14 The full-employment budget surplus:

(a) indicates the amount by which the government can decrease net taxation

(b) indicates the amount by which the government can decrease its debt

(c) is a measure of the tightness of fiscal policy

(d) (a) and (b)

3.15 Automatic stabilisers:

(a) decrease the value of the multiplier [K]

(b) decrease the height of peaks and increase the depth of troughs of income

(c) increase the height of peaks and decrease the depth of troughs of income

(d) change the timing of peaks and troughs of income

3.16 The conclusion of the balanced budget multiplier theorem is that:

(a) income cannot be at its equilibrium level if the government budget is unbalanced

(b) income cannot be at the full-employment level if the government budget is unbalanced

(c) an equal increase in exports and in imports leads to an increase in income

(d) an equal increase in net taxation and in government spending leads to an increase in income

3.17 If the level of interest rates [r] has a weak influence on investment expenditure [I], the *IS* line is:

(a) horizontal

(b) vertical

(c) steep

(d) not steep

3.18 If the level of income [Y] has a weak influence on investment expenditure [I], the *IS* line is:

(a) horizontal

(b) vertical

(c) steep

(d) not steep

3.19 If the equation of the *IS* line is:

$$r = 36 - 0.25Y$$

and the values of r and Y are:

$$r = 5.5$$

$$Y = 125$$

the real-market equilibrium process:

(a) will increase the value of Y

(b) will not change the value of Y

(c) will decrease the value of Y

(d) is impossible to predict from the information provided

3.20 The *IS* line slopes upward:

(a) when investment expenditure is greater than government expenditure

(b) when government expenditure is greater than net taxation

(c) when imports are greater than exports

(d) never

4

The Money Supply and its Determinants

This chapter is about the nature of money. The macroeconomic importance of money is indicated by the inefficiencies that occur in its absence.

One of the important features of modern money is that most of it is intangible. This is recognised in the money-supply data that are issued by the Reserve Bank of India (and by other countries' central banks). The process by which bank deposits, the dominant form of modern money, are created is described. The influences on the growth of the money supply, including both the monetary-policy role of central banks and decisions in the banks and in the rest of the private sector, are explained. The principal types of monetary policy instrument are described.

Banknotes and coins, which form a small but essential part of the money supply, are issued by central banks in whatever quantity and mix of denominations is necessary to satisfy the demand for them. A useful light-hearted reference that describes some of the economic consequences that arose when a central bank failed to do this efficiently is:

"Italy's Funny Money", *The Economist*, 15 November 1975

The key to understanding the calculations in questions 4.1 to 4.6 is the relationship between the banks' actual reserve ratio, their target reserve ratio, and the money multiplier.

Questions 4.1 and 4.2 refer to the economy whose banking system is described by the balance sheet in Box 1.

BOX 1

Rs. crore

Liabilities		Assets	
Deposits	2700	135	Reserve
		2565	Other assets
Total	2700	2700	

4.1 If the banks have been able to find borrowers for all the money they wish to lend, and the Reserve Bank of India (the central bank) sells government securities worth Rs. 1 crore to the private sector, the money supply falls by:

(a) Rs. 1 crore

(b) Rs. 5 crore

(c) Rs. 20 crore

(d) Rs. 21 crore

4.2 If the banks have not been able to find borrowers for all the money they wish to lend, the value of the money multiplier is:

(a) less than or equal to 5

(b) greater than 5

(c) less than or equal to 20

(d) greater than 20

Questions 4.3 and 4.4 refer to the economy whose banking system is described by the balance sheet in Box 2.

BOX 2

Rs. crore

Liabilities		Assets	
Deposits	1725	138	Reserve
		1587	Other assets
Total	1725	1725	

4.3 If the banks have not been able to find borrowers for all the money they wish to lend, their target reserve ratio is:

(a) less than 8%

(b) more than 8%

(c) less than 8.69%

(d) more than 8.69%

4.4 If the banks have not been able to find borrowers for all the money they wish to lend, the value of the money multiplier is:

(a) less than or equal to 12.5

(b) 12.5

(c) 11.5

(d) impossible to calculate from the information provided

Questions 4.5 and 4.6 refer to the economy whose banking system is described by the balance sheet in Box 3.

BOX 3

Rs. crore

Liabilities		Assets	
Deposits	3320	249	Reserve assets
		3071	Other assets
Total	3320	3320	

4.5 If the Reserve Bank of India (the central bank) sells government securities for Rs. 2 crore, the decrease in the value of bank deposits is:

(a) less than or equal to Rs. 26.667 crore

(b) less than Rs. 26.667 crore

(c) greater than or equal to Rs. 26.667 crore

(d) equal to Rs. 26.667 crore

4.6 If the target reserve ratio of the banks is 7%, the demand for loans is:

(a) greater than the supply of loans

(b) equal to the supply of loans
(c) less than the supply of loans
(d) less than or equal to the supply of loans

4.7 Cheques are:

(a) both money and legal tender
(b) money but not legal tender
(c) legal tender but not money
(d) neither legal tender nor money

4.8 In India, the *M4* definition of the money supply means:

(a) Indian banknotes and coins (not held by banks) and all bank deposits
(b) Indian banknotes and coins (held by banks and not held by banks) and all bank deposits
(c) Indian banknotes and coins (held by banks) and all bank deposits
(d) Indian banknotes and coins (not held by banks), all bank deposits, and Indian government securities

4.9 If bank customers withdraw Rs. 5 crore in banknotes and coins from their cheque accounts, there is:

(a) no change in the money supply
(b) an immediate change in the money supply of Rs. 5 crore
(c) a delayed change in the money supply of Rs. 5 crore
(d) a delayed change in the money supply of more than Rs. 5 crore

4.10 In India, the *M1* definition of the money supply includes:

(a) all bank deposits
(b) demand deposits
(c) banknotes and coins not held by the banks
(d) (b) and (c)

4.11 Following a deposit of cash in a bank account, the multiple creation of bank deposits occurs because:

(a) banks increase their assets (including loans) beyond the amount of cash deposited

(b) banks decrease their holding of cash to less than the amount deposited

(c) banks use their depositors' cash to buy government securities

(d) banks deposit cash at the Reserve Bank of India (the central bank) (which lends it to the government)

4.12 The money multiplier:

(a) is specified by the Reserve Bank of India (the central bank)

(b) has been abolished in the some countries

(c) is affected by open market operations

(d) depends on the demand for loans

4.13 If banks have 6.25% of their assets in reserve, and the money supply falls by Rs. 12.5 crore following a sale of securities worth Rs. 1 crore by the Reserve Bank of India (the central bank):

(a) the money multiplier has a value of 16

(b) the money multiplier has a value of greater than 16

(c) the demand for loans is less than banks can satisfy

(d) (a) and (c)

4.14 Banks' balances at the Reserve Bank of India (the central bank):

(a) increase when the central bank buys securities from the non-bank private sector

(b) decrease when the central bank buys securities from the non-bank private sector

(c) are not part of the banks' reserves

(d) are a fixed proportion of each bank's assets

4.15 If the money supply is rising, it necessarily follows that:

(a) the Reserve Bank of India (the central bank) has decided to increase the money supply

(b) prices are rising

(c) income is rising

(d) neither (a) nor (b) nor (c)

4.16 If the value of banknotes and coins in circulation is rising, it necessarily follows that:

(a) the Reserve Bank of India (the central bank) has decided to increase the money supply

(b) prices are rising

(c) income is rising

(d) neither (a) nor (b) nor (c)

4.17 Monetary policy in India means:

(a) changes in the number of Indian banknotes and coins in circulation

(b) changes in the exchange rate for the Indian rupee in terms of other currencies

(c) decisions by the Reserve Bank of India that affect the amount that Indian banks lend

(d) reducing the US government debt

4.18 An increase in the sale of government bonds by the Reserve Bank of India (the central bank) indicates that:

(a) monetary policy has been loosened

(b) fiscal policy has been loosened

(c) monetary policy has been tightened

(d) fiscal policy has been tightened

4.19 If banks decrease their target reserve ratio:

(a) there is no change in the money supply

(b) there is necessarily a multiplied increase in the money supply

(c) there might be a multiplied increase in the money supply

(d) the Reserve Bank of India (the central bank) will necessarily issue additional banknotes and coins

4.20 If banks decide to increase the proportion of their assets that are held in reserve:

(a) this is an example of monetary-policy tightening

(b) this is an example of monetary-policy loosening

(c) this causes a multiplied increase in the money supply

(d) this causes a decrease in the supply of loans

4.21 If monetary policy is tightened, there is necessarily:

(a) a decrease in the money supply

(b) a decrease in the value of banknotes and coins in circulation

(c) (a) and (b)

(d) neither (a) nor (b)

4.22 The value of the money multiplier is:

(a) greater than the reciprocal of the banks' reserve ratio

(b) greater than or equal to the reciprocal of the banks' reserve ratio

(c) less than or equal to the reciprocal of the banks' reserve ratio

(d) equal to the reciprocal of the banks' reserve ratio

4.23 An announcement by the Reserve Bank of India (the central bank) that the Benchmark Prime Lending Rate has been increased indicates a:

(a) tightening of monetary policy and a tightening of fiscal policy

(b) tightening of monetary policy and no change in fiscal policy

(c) loosening of monetary policy and a loosening of fiscal policy

(d) loosening of monetary policy and no change in fiscal policy

4.24 Assuming that the demand for loans exceeds the supply of loans, the value of the money multiplier decreases if:

(a) banks decrease their target reserve ratio

(b) banks increase their target reserve ratio

(c) the income-expenditure multiplier increases

(d) the income-expenditure multiplier decreases

4.25 The proportion of *M4* that is in the form of banknotes and coins depends on:

(a) the tightness of monetary policy

(b) the number of banknotes and coins that have been lost or destroyed

(c) the durability of banknotes and coins

(d) how companies and individuals choose to use money

4.26 Identify the decision by the Reserve Bank of India (the central bank) that tightens monetary policy:

(a) a decrease in the discount rate

(b) an increase in the discount rate

(c) a decrease in the banks' minimum reserve ratio

(d) a purchase of bonds

4.27 Measures of the money supply include bank deposits because:

(a) bank deposits are legal tender

(b) bank deposits are not legal tender

(c) cheques may be used to pay tax

(d) bank deposits are generally accepted in payment of debts

5

The *LM* Line: Income, Interest Rates, and the Money Market

This chapter explains the liquidity-preference theory of the level of interest rates [r]. The independent variables are money demand [M_D] and money supply [M_S]. Unlike the variables that were introduced in Chapter 2, these are not flow variables. M_D and M_S are measured at a moment in time. M_D is a function of the levels of income [Y] and of r. M_S is assumed not to be a function of r. Students might need to be reminded that the overwhelming majority of money is in the form of intangible bank deposits. In this chapter, exchange rates and the price level are assumed to be constant.

The *LM* line, the locus of interest-rate equilibrium combinations of Y and of r, is derived. The effects on the *LM* line of autonomous disturbances are analysed.

This chapter also describes the relationship between retail and wholesale interest rates.

The key to understanding the calculations in questions 5.1 to 5.5 is the relationship between money supply, money demand, and the equilibrium level of interest rates.

Questions 5.1 and 5.2 refer to the economy, in which the banks are experiencing an excess demand for loans, whose money sector is described by the equations in Box 4.

BOX 4

Money supply (Rs. crore)	M_S	= 900
Transactions demand for money (Rs. crore)	M_D^T	= 118 + 0.4Y
Precautionary demand for money (Rs. crore)	M_D^P	= 124 + 0.3Y
Speculative demand for money (Rs. crore)	M_D^S	= 14 – 7r
Rate of interest (%)	r	= 8

5.1 The level of income that leads to interest-rate equilibrium is:

(a) Rs. 500 crore
(b) Rs. 675 crore
(c) Rs. 998 crore
(d) Rs. 1000 crore

5.2 If the level of income increased to Rs. 1050 crore the rate of interest would increase to:

(a) 11%
(b) 12.5%
(c) 13%
(d) 13.5%

Questions 5.3 to 5.5 refer to the economy whose money sector is described by the equations in Box 5.

BOX 5

Money demand	M_D = 168 + 0.2Y – 25r
Money supply	M_S = 68

5.3 When income [Y] is equal to 1000, the equilibrium level of interest rates [r%] is:

(a) 0.8
(b) 8
(c) 12
(d) 12.5

5.4 The equation of the *LM* line is:

(a) $r = 68 + 0.2Y$

(b) $r = 4 + 0.008Y$

(c) $r = 4 + 0.08Y$

(d) impossible to calculate from the information provided

5.5 The equation of the *IS* line is:

(a) $r = 68 - 0.2Y$

(b) $r = 100 - 0.04Y$

(c) $r = 100 - 0.25Y$

(d) impossible to calculate from the information provided

5.6 When interest rates decrease:

(a) speculative demand for money increases

(b) transactions demand for money decreases

(c) precautionary demand for money increases

(d) (a) and (c)

5.7 When income increases:

(a) speculative demand for money increases

(b) transactions demand for money decreases

(c) precautionary demand for money increases

(d) (a) and (c)

5.8 When the frequency of payments decreases:

(a) speculative demand for money increases

(b) transactions demand for money decreases

(c) transactions demand for money increases

(d) (a) and (c)

5.9 To the left of the *LM* line there is disequilibrium because:

(a) the level of interest rates is rising

(b) money supply is less than money demand

(c) money supply is greater than money demand

(d) (a) and (c)

5.10 The *LM* line moves to the right if:

(a) wealth-holders believe that bond prices are going to rise

(b) income increases

(c) large employers decide to pay their employees monthly instead of weekly

(d) (a) and (c)

5.11 If the money demand function shifts

from $M_D = 88 + 0.2Y - 28r$

to $M_D = 95 + 0.3Y - 28r$

the *LM* line:

(a) shifts to the left and becomes steeper

(b) shifts to the right and becomes steeper

(c) shifts to the left and becomes less steep

(d) shifts to the right and becomes less steep

5.12 If the money supply increases, the *LM* line:

(a) shifts to the left and becomes steeper

(b) shifts to the right and becomes steeper

(c) shifts to the left with no change of gradient

(d) shifts to the right with no change of gradient

5.13 The *LM* locus identifies combinations of income and rate of interest where:

(a) money demand is equal to money supply

(b) the demand for loans is equal to the supply of loans

(c) (a) and (b)

(d) neither (a) nor (b)

5.14 Precautionary demand for money is high when:

(a) interest rates are low (and speculative demand for money is high)

(b) unemployment is high (and unemployed people have no income)

(c) bond prices are high (and capital losses are predicted)

(d) income is high (and resources are available)

5.15 If there is an increase in income, transactions demand for money increases because:

(a) interest rates change

(b) interest rates change and the exchange rate might change

(c) firms need more money in hand to pay their expenses

(d) people are less worried about unemployment

5.16 An increase in the sale of government bonds by the Reserve Bank of India (the central bank) means that:

(a) interest rates are likely to rise

(b) interest rates are likely to fall

(c) monetary policy has been tightened

(d) (a) and (c)

5.17 The speculative demand for money line [$M_D{}^S$] slopes downward because:

(a) demand for bonds is high when bond prices are low

(b) demand for bonds is high when interest rates are low

(c) demand for money is high when bond prices are low

(d) demand for money is high when interest rates are high

5.18 When interest rates are very low, the $M_D{}^S$ line is horizontal because:

(a) monetary policy is loose

(b) demand for money is zero

(c) demand for bonds is zero

(d) (a) and (b)

5.19 The *LM* line shifts downward if there is:

(a) a decrease in the money supply

(b) an increase in the sensitivity of money demand to changes in interest rates

(c) a decrease in the sensitivity of money demand to changes in interest rates

(d) (a) and (b)

5.20 The *LM* line shifts clockwise if there is:

(a) a decrease in the money supply

(b) an increase in the sensitivity of money demand to changes in interest rates

(c) an increase in the sensitivity of money demand to changes in income

(d) (a) and (b)

5.21 An *LM* line is the locus of points where:

(a) income is at the equilibrium level

(b) income is at the full-employment level

(c) the level of interest rates is stable

(d) (a) and (c)

5.22 A vertical money supply function indicates that:

(a) money includes cash (outside the banks) and bank deposits

(b) the money supply is fixed

(c) the money supply is not a function of the level of interest rates

(d) bank deposits are not legal tender

5.23 If the level of interest rates [r] has a weak influence on money demand [M_D], the *LM* line is:

(a) horizontal

(b) vertical

(c) steep

(d) not steep

5.24 If the level of income [Y] has a weak influence on money demand [M_D], the *LM* line is:

(a) horizontal

(b) vertical

(c) steep

(d) not steep

5.25 Tight monetary policy causes a:

(a) leftward shift of the money supply function and no change in the money demand function

(b) leftward shift of the money supply function and a rightward shift of the money demand function

(c) rightward shift of the money supply function and no change in the money demand function

(d) rightward shift of the money supply function and a leftward shift of the money demand function

5.26 If the economy is in the liquidity trap:

(a) monetary policy is ineffective

(b) fiscal policy is ineffective

(c) (a) and (b)

(d) neither (a) nor (b)

5.27 If the economy is in the liquidity trap, elasticity of money:

(a) demand is zero

(b) demand is infinite

(c) supply is zero

(d) supply is infinite

5.28 The liquidity preference theory of the level of interest rates refers to whether people prefer to:

(a) hold their wealth in money or in other assets

(b) hold their money in notes and coins (cash) or in bank deposits

(c) borrow or to save

(d) buy government bonds or private-sector bonds

5.29 If the equation of the *LM* line is:

$$r = -24 + 0.26Y$$

and the values of r and Y are:

$$r = 5.1$$

$$Y = 110$$

the money-market equilibrium process:

(a) will increase the value of *r*

(b) will not change the value of *r*

(c) will decrease the value of *r*

(d) is impossible to predict from the information provided

5.30 The *LM* line slopes downward:

(a) when the money supply is increasing

(b) when the money supply is stable

(c) when the money supply is decreasing

(d) never

6

The Interaction of the Goods Market and the Money Market

In this chapter, the *IS* and *LM* sub-models are integrated. These two equilibrium processes operate simultaneously and the immediate effect of each is to de-stabilise the other. As the value of Y moves towards its equilibrium value, it pushes the value of r away from its equilibrium value and *vice versa*. Students need to understand that the economy's progression towards the equilibrium at the *IS–LM* intersection is by the anti-clockwise spiral route that is described in Figure 42.

In this chapter, exchange rates and the price level are still assumed to be constant.

Simultaneous shifts of the *IS* line and of the *LM* line have indeterminate outcomes that are relevant to the understanding of the effects of autonomous changes. These include the operation of monetary policy and of fiscal policy. Also explained is the modification of the income multiplier process that follows from incorporating a variable level of interest rates into the model. Overshooting is discussed.

Students should be able to explain every part of Figure 44 and Figure 49, and to distinguish between the types of arrows that are used in each of these diagrams.

The keys to understanding the calculations in questions 6.1 to 6.19 are the aggregate-demand identity [$E_P \equiv C + I + G + (X - Z)$], the income equilibrium condition [$Y = E_P$], the interest-rate equilibrium condition [$M_D = M_S$] and the definitions of the international trade balance [$X - Z$] and of the government budget balance [$T - G$].

Questions 6.1 to 6.5 refer to the economy that is described by the equations in Box 6.

BOX 6

Disposable income (Rs. crore)	$Y_d \equiv Y - T$
Consumption expenditure (Rs. crore)	$C = 15 + 0.8Y_d$
Net taxation (Rs. crore)	$T = -5 + 0.25Y$
Investment expenditure (Rs. crore)	$I = 16 + 0.25Y - 2r$
Government expenditure (Rs. crore)	$G = 125$
Exports (Rs. crore)	$X = 110$
Imports (Rs. crore)	$Z = 120 + 0.1Y$
Rate of interest (%)	$r = 5$
Demand for money (Rs. crore)	$M_D = 20 + 0.2Y - 12r$

6.1 The equilibrium level of income is:

(a) Rs. 450 crore
(b) Rs. 500 crore
(c) Rs. 560 crore
(d) Rs. 600 crore

6.2 The value of imports when the level of income is at its equilibrium is:

(a) Rs. 66 crore
(b) Rs. 86 crore
(c) Rs. 126 crore
(d) Rs. 176 crore

6.3 The money supply is:

(a) Rs. 72 crore
(b) Rs. 80 crore
(c) Rs. 85 crore
(d) impossible to calculate from the information provided

6.4 The value of the money multiplier is:

(a) less than or equal to 8

(b) less than or equal to 10

(c) less than or equal to 12.5

(d) impossible to calculate from the information provided

6.5 The value of the income-expenditure multiplier [K] is:

(a) 4

(b) 3.5

(c) 3

(d) impossible to calculate from the information provided

Questions 6.6 to 6.10 refer to the economy that is described by the equations in Box 7

BOX 7

Disposable income (Rs. crore)	$Y_d \equiv Y - T$
Consumption expenditure (Rs. crore)	$C = 25 + 0.75Y_d$
Net taxation (Rs. crore)	$T = -20 + 0.4Y$
Investment expenditure (Rs. crore)	$I = 35 + 0.25Y - 10r$
Government expenditure (Rs. crore)	$G = 150$
Exports (Rs. crore)	$X = 200$
Imports (Rs. crore)	$Z = 125 + 0.1Y$
Money demand (Rs. crore)	$M_D = 320 + 0.2Y - 25r$
Rate of interest (%)	$r = 9$

6.6 The equilibrium level of income is:

(a) 425

(b) 475

(c) 525

(d) 575

6.7 If the interest rate is at its equilibrium level, the money supply [*Ms*] is:

(a) 200

(b) 220

(c) 290

(d) 320

6.8 The value of the income-expenditure multiplier [*K*] is:

(a) 2.5

(b) 2.75

(c) 3.0

(d) 3.25

6.9 When income is equal to 500:

(a) the government budget is in surplus

(b) the government budget is in balance

(c) the government budget is in deficit

(d) it is impossible to assess, from the information given, whether the government budget is in surplus, in balance, or in deficit

6.10 The equation of the *IS* line is:

(a) $r = 150 - 0.2Y$

(b) $r = 15 - 0.02Y$

(c) $r = 300 - 0.4Y$

(d) $r = 30 - 0.04Y$

Questions 6.11 to 6.19 refer to the economy that is described by the equations in Box 8.

BOX 8

Disposable income (Rs. crore)	$Y_d \equiv Y - T$
Consumption expenditure (Rs. crore)	$C = 30 + 0.8Y_d$
Net taxation (Rs. crore)	$T = -15 + 0.2Y$
Investment expenditure (Rs. crore)	$I = 40 - 2r$
Government expenditure (Rs. crore)	$G = 120$
Exports (Rs. crore)	$X = 135$
Imports (Rs. crore)	$Z = 115 + 0.04Y$
Money demand (Rs. crore)	$M_D = 145 + 0.2Y - 25r$
Rate of interest (%)	$r = 6$

6.11 The equilibrium level of income is:

(a) 525
(b) 575
(c) 625
(d) 675

6.12 If income is equal to 650, the money supply is:

(a) 100
(b) 125
(c) 150
(d) 175

6.13 When income is equal to 600, the international trade balance is:

(a) negative
(b) zero
(c) positive
(d) impossible to calculate from the information provided

6.14 The value of the income-expenditure multiplier [K] is:

(a) 2.5

(b) 2.75

(c) 3

(d) 3.25

6.15 The equation of the *IS* line is:

(a) $r = 222 - 0.1Y$

(b) $r = 222 - 0.2Y$

(c) $r = 111 - 0.1Y$

(d) $r = 111 - 0.2Y$

6.16 If the imports function shifts to

$$Z = 119 + 0.04Y$$

the value of the income-expenditure multiplier [K]:

(a) increases

(b) does not change

(c) decreases

(d) (a) or (c)

6.17 If the value of government expenditure shifts to

$$G = 130$$

the *IS* line shifts to the:

(a) left

(b) left and becomes steeper

(c) right

(d) right and becomes steeper

6.18 If the money demand function shifts to

$$M_D = 145 + 0.2Y - 15r$$

the *LM* line shifts:

(a) upward (to the left) and becomes steeper

(b) downward (to the right) and becomes steeper

(c) upward (to the left) and becomes less steep

(d) downward (to the right) and becomes less steep

6.19 The equation for investment expenditure in Box 8 does not include a multiple of Y. This implies that:

(a) there is a printing error in this book

(b) income is at the full-employment level

(c) all the existing machinery is in use

(d) in this economy, investment is not affected by changes in income

6.20 A change in the level of interest rates causes a shift of:

(a) the *IS* line

(b) the graph showing the effect of income [Y] on investment spending [I]

(c) the graph showing the effect of interest rates [r] on investment spending [I]

(d) the graph showing the effect of interest rates [r] on speculative demand for money [M_D^S]

6.21 A tight fiscal policy combined with a loose monetary policy leads to:

(a) a decrease in income and a decrease in interest rates

(b) a decrease in income and an increase in interest rates

(c) a decrease in income and an indeterminate change in interest rates

(d) an indeterminate change in income and a decrease in interest rates

6.22 An increase in the sensitivity of investment to changes in the level of interest rates:

(a) makes the *IS* line steeper

(b) makes the *IS* line less steep

(c) shifts the *LM* line to the left

(d) shifts the *LM* line to the right

6.23 To the left of the *IS* line there is disequilibrium because:

(a) money supply is greater than money

(b) money supply is less than money demand

(c) planned injections are greater than withdrawals

(d) planned injections are less than withdrawals

6.24 Assuming that there is no change in the money supply, an increased level of government spending:

(a) decreases the level of interest rates

(b) increases the level of interest rates

(c) has no effect on the level of interest rates

(d) (a) or (b)

6.25 A change in the level of income causes a shift of:

(a) the *IS* line

(b) the *LM* line

(c) the graph showing the effect of interest rates [r] on investment spending [I]

(d) the graph showing the effect of income [Y] on transactions demand for money [$M_D{}^T$]

6.26 Following a change in autonomous expenditure, the new equilibrium level of income is likely to be:

(a) reached without a change in interest rates

(b) reached with a change in interest rates

(c) an objective of the government

(d) at or near full employment

6.27 The value of the income-expenditure multiplier [K] depends on:

(a) the money multiplier

(b) the amount of government spending

(c) the marginal propensity to import

(d) the size of the government budget deficit

6.28 When income increases:

(a) consumption expenditure increases

(b) investment expenditure decreases

(c) the *IS* line shifts

(d) the *LM* line shifts

6.29 When interest rates increase:

(a) consumption expenditure increases

(b) investment expenditure decreases

(c) the *IS* line shifts

(d) the *LM* line shifts

6.30 If the Reserve Bank of India (the central bank) sells securities to the private sector at the same time that net taxes are increased, this is an example of:

(a) loose monetary policy and loose fiscal policy

(b) loose monetary policy and tight fiscal policy

(c) tight monetary policy and loose fiscal policy

(d) tight monetary policy and tight fiscal policy

6.31 If the Reserve Bank of India (the central bank) sells securities to the private sector at the same time that net taxes are increased, the effect is:

(a) a decrease in income and a decrease in interest rates

(b) a decrease in income and an increase in interest rates

(c) a decrease in income and an indeterminate effect on interest rates

(d) an increase in income and a decrease in interest rates

6.32 An autonomous increase in investment expenditure leads to:

(a) an increase in the rate of interest and an increase in income

(b) an increase in the rate of interest and a decrease in income

(c) a decrease in the rate of interest and an increase in income

(d) a decrease in the rate of interest and a decrease in income

6.33 An autonomous increase in the money supply leads to:

(a) an increase in the rate of interest and an increase in income

(b) an increase in the rate of interest and a decrease in income

(c) a decrease in the rate of interest and an increase in income

(d) a decrease in the rate of interest and a decrease in income

6.34 In order to reach the final equilibrium, if the values of income and of interest rates are on the *IS* line but above the *LM* line, income:

(a) increases and interest rates increase

(b) increases and interest rates decrease

(c) decreases and interest rates increase

(d) decreases and interest rates decrease

6.35 If there is a decrease in the level of interest rates, speculative demand for money increases because:

(a) wealth holders sell bonds to realise capital gains

(b) the *LM* line shifts

(c) the *IS* line shifts

(d) lower interest rates encourage increased investment

6.36 If a government budget deficit is financed by borrowing (issuing bonds):

(a) the *LM* line shifts and the *IS* line does not shift

(b) the *IS* line shifts and the *LM* line does not shift

(c) the *LM* line shifts and the *IS* line shifts

(d) neither the *LM* line shifts nor the *IS* line shifts

6.37 The formula for the income-expenditure multiplier [K] assumes that the level of interest rates is constant. If interest rates are not constant, the value of the multiplier:

(a) increases

(b) does not change

(c) decreases

(d) might increase or decrease or neither

6.38 An increase in the marginal propensity to consume makes the:

(a) *IS* line steeper

(b) *IS* line less steep

(c) *LM* line steeper

(d) *LM* line less steep

6.39 An example of overshooting is:

(a) there is a delay before an increase in interest rates moderates the effect on income of an increase in exports

(b) interest rates are too high to stimulate sufficient investment to keep the economy at full employment

(c) following a budget deficit, the government cuts its expenditure and causes substantial unemployment

(d) imports are greater than exports, so unemployment increases

6.40 A variable level of interest rates:

(a) increases the income-expenditure multiplier

(b) does not change the income-expenditure multiplier

(c) decreases the income-expenditure multiplier

(d) (a) or (b)

Questions 6.41 to 6.44 refer to the immediate relationships in the Keynesian model. The notation is in Box 9.

BOX 9

I	investment expenditure
J	injections
M_D	money demand
M_D^S	speculative money demand
M_D^T	transactions money demand
M_S	money supply
S	savings
W	withdrawals
Z	imports

6.41 The level of interest rates immediately affects:

(a) I and M_D^S but not M_D^T

(b) M_D^S and M_D^T but not I

(c) I and M_D^T but not M_D^S

(d) I and M_D^S and M_D^T

6.42 The level of income immediately affects:

(a) I and S but not Z

(b) I and Z but not S

(c) S and Z but not I

(d) S and Z and I

6.43 The equilibrium level of income is immediately affected by:

(a) M_S and J but not W

(b) M_S and W but not J

(c) W and J but not M_S

(d) M_S and J and W

6.44 The equilibrium level of interest rates is immediately affected by:

(a) I and M_D but not M_S

(b) M_S and M_D but not I

(c) I and M_S but not M_D

(d) M_D and M_S and I

6.45 Tight fiscal policy:

(a) increases Y and increases r

(b) increases Y and decreases r

(c) decreases Y and decreases r

(d) decreases Y and increases r

6.46 Tight monetary policy:

(a) increases Y and increases r

(b) increases Y and decreases r

(c) decreases Y and decreases r

(d) decreases Y and increases r

6.47 If the goods market is in equilibrium but the money market is not in equilibrium, the combination of values of Y and of r is:

(a) on the *IS* line

(b) on the *LM* line

(c) (a) and (b)

(d) neither (a) nor (b)

6.48 If the equation of the *IS* line is

$$r = 25 - 0.2Y$$

and the equation of the *LM* line is

$$r = -35 + 0.4Y$$

and the values of r and Y are

$$r = 4.5$$
$$Y = 110$$

(a) Y will increase and r will decrease

(b) Y will increase and r will increase

(c) Y will decrease and r will increase

(d) neither (a) nor (b) nor (c)

6.49 On an *IS–LM* diagram, the path towards the simultaneous equilibrium values of Y and r is shown as:

(a) a clockwise spiral

(b) an anti-clockwise spiral

(c) a straight line

(d) neither (a) nor (b) nor (c)

7

Digression on Pre-Keynesian Economic Theory

This chapter introduces students to the key aspects of the Classical macroeconomic theory, some parts of which are of increasing current importance. Comparisons between theoretical approaches are important. The Classical theory emphasises the importance of price incentives (including interest-rate incentives). It also assumes a very limited economic role for governments. Later chapters of *Interest Rates, Prices, and the Economy* refer to other parts of the Classical macroeconomic theory.

Say's Law, the loanable-funds theory of the level of interest rates, and the Classical view of unemployment are explained. In each case, the Keynesian response is also discussed.

7.1 The doctrine of *laissez-faire* is that:

(a) poor people deserve to be poor

(b) rich people deserve to be rich

(c) governments should not intervene in the macroeconomy

(d) (b) and (c)

7.2 Prices that are "sticky":

(a) might not adjust by enough to achieve the demand-supply equilibrium

(b) never adjust by enough to achieve the demand-supply equilibrium

(c) adjust slowly and reach the demand-supply equilibrium in the long term

(d) adjust by more than is needed and overshoot the demand-supply equilibrium

7.3 According to the Classical theory, unemployment does not persist because:

(a) interest rates are low

(b) taxes are low

(c) wage rates are flexible

(d) wage rates are not flexible

7.4 Say's Law states that:

(a) demand creates supply

(b) demand is equal to supply

(c) supply creates demand

(d) supply is not related to demand

7.5 According to the Classical theory, the supply of loanable funds [S_{LF}] is determined by:

(a) interest rates

(b) income

(c) confidence

(d) (b) and (c)

7.6 According to the Classical theory, the demand for loanable funds [D_{LF}] is determined by:

(a) interest rates

(b) income

(c) confidence

(d) (b) and (c)

7.7 According to the Classical theory, the full-employment level of output:

(a) should be a government objective

(b) never occurs

(c) is the equilibrium

(d) occurs if interest rates are stable

7.8 According to the Classical theory, when the supply of a commodity is not equal to the demand for it, its price responds:

(a) quickly, and is a powerful influence on human behaviour

(b) quickly, and might be a weak influence on human behaviour

(c) very slowly, and is a powerful influence on human behaviour

(d) very slowly, and might be a weak influence on human behaviour

7.9 According to the Classical theory, the level of consumption expenditure [C] is determined by the level of:

(a) interest rates [r]

(b) income [Y]

(c) (a) and (b)

(d) neither (a) nor (b)

7.10 According to the Keynesian theory, the level of consumption expenditure [C] is determined by the level of:

(a) interest rates (r)

(b) income (Y)

(c) (a) and (b)

(d) neither (a) nor (b)

8

The Role of the Price Level in Aggregate Demand and Supply

In this chapter, an additional independent variable, the price level [*P*], is introduced into the model. The intersection of the aggregate demand line [*AD*] and aggregate supply line [*AS*] simultaneously determines the levels of income [*Y*] and of prices. The *AD* line is derived from the *IS–LM* diagram. The Classical and Keynesian views of the *AS* line, and the Classical and Keynesian outcomes of the *AD–AS* model, are explained. In this chapter, exchange rates are still assumed to be constant.

The nature and consequences of shifts of the *AD* line and of the *AS* line are analysed. Simultaneous shifts of these two lines have indeterminate consequences.

8.1 An increase in the price level shifts the *LM* line to the left because:

(a) net exports decrease

(b) investment increases

(c) the real money supply is decreased

(d) full employment is not possible

8.2 An increase in the price level shifts the *IS* line to the left because:

(a) net exports decrease

(b) investment increases

(c) the real money supply is decreased

(d) full employment is not possible

8.3 The *AD* line shifts to the right if:

(a) government spending [G] decreases

(b) autonomous net tax revenue [v] decreases

(c) the rate of interest [r] decreases

(d) (b) and (c)

8.4 If the *AD* line shifts to the right, the price level [P]:

(a) increases

(b) remains the same

(c) increases or remains the same

(d) decreases

8.5 If the *AD* line shifts to the right:

(a) income increases

(b) income does not change

(c) income decreases

(d) additional information is needed to predict the change in income

8.6 An increase in the real money supply has occurred if:

(a) the Reserve Bank of India (the central bank) has issued a greater value of banknotes and coins than it has withdrawn

(b) the Reserve Bank of India (the central bank) has issued a smaller value of banknotes and coins than it has withdrawn

(c) the percentage increase in *M4* is greater than the percentage increase in *M1*

(d) the percentage increase in the nominal money supply is greater than the percentage increase in the price level

8.7 An increase in government expenditure [G] leads to:

(a) an increase in the price level

(b) no change in the price level

(c) a decrease in the price level

(d) (a) or (b)

8.8 According to the Keynesian approach, an increase in aggregate demand:

(a) has no effect on the price level

(b) causes the price level to rise

(c) might cause the price level to rise

(d) might cause the price level to fall

8.9 According to the Classical approach, an increase in aggregate demand:

(a) has no effect on the price level

(b) causes the price level to rise

(c) might cause the price level to rise

(d) might cause the price level to fall

8.10 The aggregate supply line [*AS*] is horizontal if:

(a) prices are flexible

(b) income is at the full-employment level [Y_{FE}]

(c) interest rates are falling

(d) an increase in aggregate demand does not increase the price level

8.11 A shift of the aggregate supply line to the right is caused by an increase in:

(a) equilibrium output [Y_e]

(b) maximum output [Y_{FE}]

(c) the money supply [M_S]

(d) the price level [P]

8.12 A shift of the aggregate supply line upward is caused by an increase in:

(a) equilibrium output

(b) maximum output

(c) business costs

(d) aggregate demand

8.13 If the *AD* line shifts to the right and the *AS* line shifts upward:

(a) income increases and the price level increases

(b) income increases and the price level might increase or decrease

(c) the price level increases and income might increase or decrease

(d) the price level increases and income decreases

8.14 An increase in the price of imports:

(a) shifts the *AD* line to the left

(b) shifts the *AS* line upward

(c) shifts the *AS* line to the left

(d) (b) and (c)

8.15 When the nominal money supply is constant and the price level increases:

(a) the real money supply increases

(b) the real money supply remains the same

(c) the real money supply decreases

(d) it is impossible to predict, from the information given, the direction of the change in the real money supply

8.16 If both the goods market and the money market are in equilibrium:

(a) the combination of values of Y and of r is on the *IS* line but not on the *LM* line

(b) the combination of values of Y and of P is on the *AD* line

(c) (a) and (b)

(d) neither (a) nor (b)

8.17 If the *AD* line shifts to the right when income is at the full-employment level [Y_{FE}]:

(a) income decreases and there is no change in the price level

(b) income increases and there is no change in the price level

(c) the price level decreases and there is no change in income

(d) the price level increases and there is no change in income

8.18 If the *AD* line shifts to the right during a severe depression:

(a) income decreases and there is no change in the price level

(b) income increases and there is no change in the price level

(c) the price level decreases and there is no change in income

(d) the price level increases and there is no change in income

9

Inflation: Causes, Effects, Policy

This is an applied chapter in which theory is utilised. There are many types of inflation, which may be categorised by speed and by cause. Inflation does not simply mean increases in the price level. Hyper-inflation is considered briefly and attention is then concentrated on creeping inflation.

Demand-pull inflation and cost-push inflation cause or encourage each other. Depressions are caused by the inverse of the demand-pull inflation process, so are also considered in this chapter. Cost-push inflation might be associated with depression conditions.

The effects of several types of anti-inflation policy are considered. In many cases, the rate of inflation is decreased at the cost of causing or intensifying other problems. Anti-depression policy is also discussed.

Also discussed in this chapter are the Fisher equation, the Phillips curve, and the Classical and monetarist views on inflation.

9.1 During a period of inflation:

(a) all prices increase and the price level increases

(b) all prices increase at the same rate and the price level increases

(c) many prices increase and the price level increases

(d) many prices increase but the price level does not increase

9.2 Demand-pull inflation occurs when aggregate demand is greater than:

(a) output

(b) planned output
(c) full-employment output
(d) full-employment output (excluding the government sector)

9.3 During a period of demand-pull inflation:
(a) unemployment is high
(b) unemployment is low
(c) all prices increase
(d) (a) or (b)

9.4 During a period of cost-push inflation:
(a) unemployment is high
(b) unemployment is low
(c) all prices increase
(d) (a) or (b)

9.5 The Phillips curve:
(a) shows that inflation causes high unemployment
(b) shows that high unemployment causes inflation
(c) never shifts
(d) neither (a) nor (b) nor (c)

9.6 Unemployment cannot be caused by:
(a) demand-pull inflation
(b) cost-push inflation
(c) tight fiscal policy
(d) tight monetary policy

9.7 Fiscal drag means that an effect of a progressive system of taxation is that:
(a) high net tax rates decrease disposable income
(b) real net tax revenue is constant
(c) net tax revenue rises at least as fast as the price level
(d) net tax revenue increases faster than the price level

9.8 An effect of demand-pull inflation is to:

(a) increase the demand for imports
(b) decrease the demand for imports
(c) increase the demand for exports
(d) (a) and (c)

9.9 During a period of demand-pull inflation:

(a) the incentive to save increases
(b) the incentive to save decreases
(c) there is no effect on the incentive to save
(d) (a) or (c)

9.10 During a period of cost-push inflation, monetary policy:

(a) is not relevant
(b) should be loose
(c) should be tight
(d) is not permitted

9.11 During a period of cost-push inflation, statutory price and wage controls are:

(a) always successful
(b) probably successful
(c) probably successful in the short term only
(d) never successful

9.12 During a severe depression, a loose fiscal policy:

(a) increases interest rates, and increases the price level
(b) increases interest rates, and has no effect on the price level
(c) has no effect on interest rates, and increases the price level
(d) has no effect on interest rates, and has no effect on the price level

9.13 During a period of demand-pull inflation, a tight fiscal policy:

(a) decreases interest rates, and decreases the price level
(b) decreases interest rates, and has no effect on the price level

(c) has no effect on interest rates, and decreases the price level

(d) has no effect on interest rates, and has no effect on the price level

9.14 According to the Classical theory:

(a) an increase in the money supply causes a decrease in interest rates

(b) increases in the price level are proportional to increases in the money supply

(c) increases in the velocity of circulation are proportional to increases in the money supply

(d) (a) and (b)

9.15 According to the Keynesian theory:

(a) an increase in the money supply causes a decrease in interest rates

(b) increases in the price level are proportional to increases in the money supply

(c) increases in the velocity of circulation are proportional to increases in the money supply

(d) (a) and (b)

9.16 A vertical long-run Phillips curve implies that:

(a) unemployment tends towards a rate that can co-exist with any inflation rate

(b) inflation tends towards a rate that can co-exist with any unemployment rate

(c) the unemployment rate is constant

(d) the unemployment rate cannot be equal to zero

9.17 Demand-pull inflation:

(a) cannot occur simultaneously with cost-push inflation

(b) tends to discourage cost-push inflation

(c) tends to encourage cost-push inflation

(d) tends to encourage cost-push inflation and *vice versa*

9.18 When the price level is increasing, the economy is experiencing fiscal drag if net tax revenue:

(a) is constant

(b) increases more slowly than the price level

(c) increases at the same rate as the price level

(d) increases faster than the price level

10

Unemployment : Causes, Effects, Policy

This is an applied chapter that emphasises that unemployment is more complex than was implied in the discussion of depression conditions in Chapter 9. The difficulties of measuring and classifying unemployment are discussed. Four types of unemployment, and relevant policies, are explained. There is also a brief discussion of the target level of measured unemployment.

10.1 Full employment:

(a) occurs if the economy is at the equilibrium level of output

(b) never occurs

(c) never occurs spontaneously

(d) neither (a) nor (b) nor (c)

10.2 Full employment means that:

(a) everyone is working

(b) everyone who wishes to work is working

(c) everyone who is able to work is working

(d) neither (a) nor (b) nor (c)

10.3 Structural unemployment might occur because:

(a) people have irrelevant skills

(b) fiscal policy is tight

(c) unemployed people do not know where the vacancies are

(d) (a) and (b)

10.4 Frictional unemployment might occur because:

(a) people have irrelevant skills

(b) fiscal policy is tight

(c) unemployed people do not know where the vacancies are

(d) (a) and (c)

10.5 An increase in unemployment:

(a) increases net taxation

(b) does not change net taxation

(c) decreases net taxation

(d) (b) or (c)

10.6 Keynesian (insufficient demand) unemployment increases if:

(a) the *IS* line shifts to the right

(b) the *LM* line shifts to the left

(c) (a) and (b)

(d) neither (a) nor (b)

10.7 The Phillips curve implies that:

(a) the relationship between inflation and unemployment never changes

(b) a low inflation rate might be a necessary condition for a reduction in the unemployment rate

(c) a high unemployment rate might be a necessary condition for a reduction in the inflation rate

(d) (a) and (c)

10.8 The occurrence of unemployment necessarily indicates that:

(a) production methods are efficient

(b) output has been foregone

(c) interest rates are high

(d) neither (a) nor (b) nor (c)

10.9 The occurrence of full employment necessarily indicates that:

(a) production methods are efficient

(b) output has been foregone

(c) interest rates are high

(d) neither (a) nor (b) nor (c)

11

Exchange Rates and International Payments

The international sector is introduced in this applied chapter. The nature of international payments and of the balance of payments are explained. International trade is only one of the many reasons for international payments. Short-term and long-term capital movements and other payments might also be substantial.

Several types of each of fixed and floating exchange rate systems, and their advantages and disadvantages, are explained. The intended and actual effects of devaluations (under a fixed exchange rate) are described. Revaluations are also mentioned. The need for reserves, and the fact that insufficient reserves might make a fixed exchange rate system unsustainable, are explained. A discussion of recent monetary developments in western Europe illustrates some of the key issues.

Nominal and real exchange rates are defined in this chapter.

11.1 In a country with a fixed exchange rate, an excess demand for local currency (in exchange for foreign currency) leads to:

(a) appreciation of the local currency

(b) an increase in the money supply

(c) a devaluation

(d) an increase in interest rates

11.2 In a country with a clean floating exchange rate, an excess demand for local currency (in exchange for foreign currency) leads to:

(a) appreciation of the local currency

(b) an increase in the money supply

(c) a devaluation

(d) an increase in interest rates

11.3 In a country with a fixed exchange rate, assuming that there is neither a devaluation nor a revaluation nor monetary sterilisation, an excess demand for local currency (in exchange for foreign currency) leads to a shift of the:

(a) *IS* line

(b) *LM* line

(c) (a) and (b)

(d) neither (a) nor (b)

11.4 In a country with a clean floating exchange rate, an excess demand for local currency (in exchange for foreign currency) leads to a shift of the:

(a) *IS* line

(b) *LM* line

(c) (a) and (b)

(d) neither (a) nor (b)

11.5 In a country with a fixed exchange rate:

(a) the level of interest rates is stable

(b) the money supply is stable

(c) monetary policy is ineffective

(d) the exchange rate never changes

11.6 In a country with a fixed exchange rate, a balance of payments deficit necessarily leads to:

(a) a devaluation

(b) an increase in net taxation

(c) a decrease in the money supply

(d) an increase in income

11.7 In a country with a clean floating exchange rate, a balance of payments deficit necessarily leads to:

(a) depreciation of the local currency

(b) a decrease in net taxation

(c) a decrease in the money supply

(d) a decrease in income

11.8 In a country with a fixed exchange rate:

(a) the value of the local currency never changes

(b) the value of the local currency never increases but might decrease

(c) any increase in the value of the local currency during one day is matched by an equal decrease in its value the following day

(d) neither (a) nor (b) nor (c)

11.9 In a country with a fixed exchange rate, assuming that there is neither a devaluation nor a revaluation nor monetary sterilisation, a balance of payments deficit necessarily leads to:

(a) appreciation of the local currency

(b) depreciation of the local currency

(c) a decrease in the money supply

(d) an increase in the money supply

11.10 In a country with a fixed exchange rate, assuming that there is neither a devaluation nor a revaluation nor monetary sterilisation, a balance of payments deficit necessarily leads to:

(a) an increase in net taxation

(b) a decrease in net taxation

(c) a shift of the *LM* line

(d) neither (a) nor (b) nor (c)

11.11 In a country with a clean floating exchange rate, a balance of payments deficit necessarily leads to:

(a) an increase in net taxation

(b) a decrease in net taxation

(c) a shift of the *LM* line

(d) neither (a) nor (b) nor (c)

11.12 In a country with a fixed exchange rate:

(a) fiscal policy is not effective

(b) monetary policy is not effective

(c) prices and incomes policy is not effective

(d) (a) and (b)

11.13 Appreciation of the real exchange rate might be caused by:

(a) depreciation of the nominal exchange rate

(b) a decrease in the price level of domestic output

(c) a decrease in the price level of output in other countries

(d) (a) and/or (b)

11.14 The Indian real exchange rate is a:

(a) trade-weighted average of exchange rates with respect to other currencies

(b) measure of the purchasing power of the Indian rupee

(c) measure of the competitiveness of Indian output in other countries

(d) measure of the degree of open-ness of the Indian economy

11.15 "Hot Money" moves across international boundaries:

(a) to pay for imports and exports

(b) in response to changes in interest rates

(c) to buy physical assets (including land)

(d) to finance the illegal drug trade

11.16 If the value of a currency decreases, that country's *IS* line shifts:

(a) to the right

(b) to the left

(c) to the right if demand for net exports is inelastic

(d) to the left if demand for net exports is inelastic

11.17 In a country with a managed floating exchange rate:

(a) intervention in the currency market by the central bank always prevents severe exchange-rate fluctuation

(b) the ability of the central bank to use intervention to prevent severe exchange-rate fluctuation depends on the accuracy of short-term forecasting

(c) the central bank does not intervene in the currency market

(d) the balance of trade is always equal to zero

11.18 A revaluation, in a country with a fixed exchange rate:

(a) decreases unemployment

(b) decreases the price of exports

(c) decreases the price of imports

(d) causes cost-push inflation

11.19 The effectiveness of a devaluation, in a country with a fixed exchange rate, depends on:

(a) whether other relevant countries also devalue

(b) the elasticity of demand for net exports

(c) (a) and (b)

(d) neither (a) nor (b)

11.20 Countries that have adopted the euro as their currency expect to benefit from:

(a) stable US-dollar exchange rates

(b) low interest rates

(c) decreased transactions costs

(d) (b) and (c)

11.21 Demand for imports is inelastic if the percentage increase in demand for imports is:

(a) greater than the percentage decrease in price of imports

(b) greater than the percentage decrease in price of exports

(c) less than the percentage decrease in price of imports

(d) less than the percentage decrease in price of exports

11.22 If the demand for imports is inelastic, an increase in the price of imports:

(a) shifts the *IS* line to the left

(b) shifts the *IS* line to the right

(c) rotates the *IS* line clockwise

(d) does not affect the *IS* line

11.23 If the demand for imports is inelastic, an increase in the price of imports:

(a) shifts the *LM* line to the left

(b) shifts the *LM* line to the right

(c) rotates the *LM* line clockwise

(d) does not affect the *LM* line

11.24 The experience of the European Monetary System in 1992 illustrates that:

(a) fixed exchange rates are necessarily unsustainable

(b) high interest rates decrease investment

(c) a fixed exchange rate precludes an independent monetary policy

(d) (a) and (c)

11.25 The effect of a creeping-peg exchange-rate system is:

(a) short-term flexibility and long-term stability

(b) long-term flexibility and short-term stability

(c) long-term flexibility and long-term stability

(d) short-term flexibility and short-term stability

11.26 In a country with a clean floating exchange rate:

(a) there are no devaluations

(b) the central bank does not intervene in the currency market

(c) (a) and (b)

(d) neither (a) nor (b)

11.27 In a country with a dirty floating exchange rate:

(a) there are no devaluations

(b) the central bank does not intervene in the currency market

(c) (a) and (b)

(d) neither (a) nor (b)

11.28 In a country with an adjustable peg:

(a) there are no devaluations

(b) the central bank does not intervene in the currency market

(c) (a) and (b)

(d) neither (a) nor (b)

11.29 In a country with a creeping peg:

(a) there are no devaluations

(b) the central bank does not intervene in the currency market

(c) (a) and (b)

(d) neither (a) nor (b)

11.30 A managed floating exchange rate is also known as:

(a) an adjustable peg

(b) a creeping peg

(c) a dirty floating exchange rate

(d) a clean floating exchange rate

11.31 If, under a fixed exchange rate, there is a sudden deterioration in the balance of payments (but no devaluation), and the monetary effect is sterilised:

(a) the central bank sells securities

(b) the central bank buys securities

(c) net taxation is decreased

(d) net taxation is increased

12

The *BP* Line: Income, Interest Rates, and the Currency Market

In this chapter, the balance of payments constraint is added to the *IS–LM* model. The outcome of this model changes if there is a non-zero balance of payments. The *BP* line describes the relationship between the balance of payments and the levels of income and of interest rates. Superimposing the *BP* line on the *IS–LM* diagram frequently leads to powerful conclusions.

The *BP* line is an equilibrium locus if the exchange rate is floating but not otherwise. A fixed exchange rate means that the money supply changes, and the *LM* line shifts, if the balance of payments is not equal to zero. A floating exchange rate means that the exchange rate changes if the balance of payments is not equal to zero. This changes import prices and export prices and, depending on their effects on demand for net exports, might cause the *IS* line to shift. The direction of the net shift of the *IS* line depends on the elasticities of demand for exports and for imports.

The *IS–LM–BP* diagram is used to show the effects of a balance of payments deficit or surplus. The outcome depends on the nature of the exchange-rate system, the elasticities of demand for exports and for imports, the international mobility of capital, and the perceived likelihood of stability of the local currency. Several combinations that lead to unstable situations are identified.

The effectiveness of fiscal policy and of monetary policy when combined with each of fixed and floating exchange rates is discussed.

The keys to understanding the calculations in questions 12.39 to 12.41 are the definition of the balance of payments and the significance of the *IS–LM* intersection.

12.1 A *BP* line is the locus of points where:

(a) the balance of payments is equal to zero

(b) the balance of trade is equal to zero

(c) net international capital inflow is equal to zero

(d) (a) and (b)

12.2 In a country with a fixed exchange rate, assuming that there is neither a devaluation nor a revaluation nor monetary sterilisation, monetary policy is ineffective because:

(a) inflation decreases the purchasing power of the currency unit

(b) the government might decide to pay its debts with newly-issued money

(c) high interest rates attract an inflow of capital

(d) the government is the residual buyer or seller in the currency market

12.3 In a country with a floating exchange rate, fiscal policy is probably ineffective because:

(a) net tax revenue is partly a function of income

(b) the nominal exchange rate influences the real exchange rate

(c) the income-expenditure multiplier [K] is not constant

(d) the money multiplier is not constant

12.4 In a country with a floating exchange rate and infinite mobility of capital, an increase in exports combined with a change by major employers from weekly to monthly wage payments leads to:

(a) an increase in income and an increase in the rate of interest

(b) an increase in income and no change in the rate of interest

(c) a decrease in income and an increase in the rate of interest

(d) a decrease in income and no change in the rate of interest

12.5 In a country with a floating exchange rate and infinite mobility of capital, monetary policy, as a device to influence the level of income, is effective because:

(a) inflation decreases the purchasing power of the currency unit

(b) the government might decide to pay its debts by selling assets

(c) high interest rates attract an inflow of capital and *vice versa*

(d) the government is the residual buyer or seller in the currency market

12.6 In a country with a fixed exchange rate and infinite international capital mobility, assuming that there is neither a devaluation nor a revaluation nor monetary sterilisation, fiscal policy is:

(a) effective and monetary policy is ineffective

(b) effective and monetary policy is effective

(c) ineffective and monetary policy is ineffective

(d) ineffective and monetary policy is effective

12.7 In a country with a floating exchange rate and infinite international capital mobility, fiscal policy is:

(a) effective and monetary policy is ineffective

(b) effective and monetary policy is effective

(c) ineffective and monetary policy is ineffective

(d) ineffective and monetary policy is effective

12.8 A *BP* line that is horizontal indicates that an increase in interest rates causes:

(a) zero net international capital flow

(b) an infinite international inflow of capital

(c) a very small international inflow of capital

(d) an infinite international outflow of capital

12.9 The effect of a *BP* line that is horizontal is that:

(a) interest rates are at the same level as foreign interest rates

(b) the money supply does not change

(c) the money supply does not change if there is a non-zero balance of payments

(d) the exchange rate does not change

12.10 In a country with a fixed exchange rate and infinite international capital mobility, assuming that there is neither a devaluation nor a revaluation nor monetary sterilization, an autonomous increase in the money supply causes:

(a) an increase in income and no change in interest rates

(b) an increase in income and a decrease in interest rates

(c) no change in income and no change in interest rates

(d) a decrease in income and no change in interest rates

12.11 In a country with a floating exchange rate and infinite international capital mobility, an autonomous increase in the money supply causes:

(a) an increase in income and no change in interest rates

(b) an increase in income and a decrease in interest rates

(c) no change in income and no change in interest rates

(d) a decrease in income and no change in interest rates

12.12 A *BP* line that is vertical might indicate that:

(a) changes in local interest rates [*r*] do not affect the net international capital outflow (*F*)

(b) international capital flows are not permitted

(c) changes in income [*Y*] do not affect expenditure on imports [*Z*]

(d) (a) and (b)

12.13 In a country with a floating exchange rate that is perceived to be likely to be stable, assuming that international capital mobility is less than infinite, depreciation causes the *BP* line to shift:

(a) upward

(b) downward

(c) clockwise

(d) anti-clockwise

12.14 In a country with a floating exchange rate, assuming that international capital is infinitely mobile, the gradient of the *BP* line is:

(a) zero

(b) greater than zero but less than infinity

(c) infinity

(d) impossible to calculate from the information provided

12.15 In a country with a floating exchange rate, assuming that international capital is less than infinitely mobile, the gradient of the *BP* line is:

(a) zero

(b) greater than zero but less than infinity

(c) infinity

(d) impossible to calculate from the information provided

12.16 In a country with a fixed exchange rate, assuming that the mobility of international capital is less than infinite but greater than zero, and assuming that there is neither a devaluation nor a revaluation nor monetary sterilisation, the gradient of the *BP* line is:

(a) zero

(b) greater than zero but less than infinity

(c) infinity

(d) impossible to calculate from the information provided

12.17 In a country with a floating exchange rate, appreciation causes the *IS* line to shift to the left:

(a) if the demand for imports is elastic

(b) if the demand for imports is inelastic

(c) whether the demand for imports is elastic or inelastic

(d) neither (a) nor (b) nor (c)

12.18 In a country with a floating exchange rate, appreciation causes the *LM* line to shift to the left:

(a) if the demand for imports is elastic

(b) if the demand for imports is inelastic

(c) whether the demand for imports is elastic or inelastic

(d) neither (a) nor (b) nor (c)

12.19 In a country with a floating exchange rate, the *BP* line is the locus of combinations of *r* and *Y* where:

(a) the price level is stable

(b) the exchange rate is in equilibrium

(c) the balance of payments is equal to zero

(d) (b) and (c)

12.20 In a country with a fixed exchange rate, assuming that there is neither a devaluation nor a revaluation nor monetary sterilisation, the *BP* line is the locus of combinations of *r* and *Y* where:

(a) the price level is stable

(b) the exchange rate is in equilibrium

(c) the balance of payments is equal to zero

(d) (b) and (c)

12.21 In a country with a floating exchange rate, a balance of payments deficit causes a shift of:

(a) the *IS* line but not the *LM* line

(b) the *LM* line but not the *IS* line

(c) the *IS* line and/or the *LM* line

(d) neither the *IS* line nor the *LM* line

12.22 In a country with a fixed exchange rate, assuming that there is neither a devaluation nor a revaluation nor monetary sterilisation, a balance of payments deficit causes a shift of:

(a) the *IS* line but not the *LM* line

(b) the *LM* line but not the *IS* line

(c) the *IS* line and/or the *LM* line

(d) neither the *IS* line nor the *LM* line

12.23 If a country with a floating exchange rate has a balance of payments deficit, the perceived stability or instability of the currency determines the direction of the shift of:

(a) the *IS* line but not the *BP* line

(b) the *BP* line but not the *IS* line

(c) the *IS* line and/or the *BP* line

(d) neither the *IS* line nor the *BP* line

12.24 If a country with a fixed exchange rate has a balance of payments deficit, assuming that there is neither a devaluation nor a revaluation nor monetary sterilisation, the perceived stability or instability of the currency determines the direction of the shift of:

(a) the *IS* line but not the *BP* line

(b) the *BP* line but not the *IS* line

(c) the *IS* line and/or the *BP* line

(d) neither the *IS* line nor the *BP* line

Questions 12.25 to 12.27 refer to the economy that is described in the graph in Box 10. A government decision causes the shift in the LM line. The shift in the IS line follows.

BOX 10

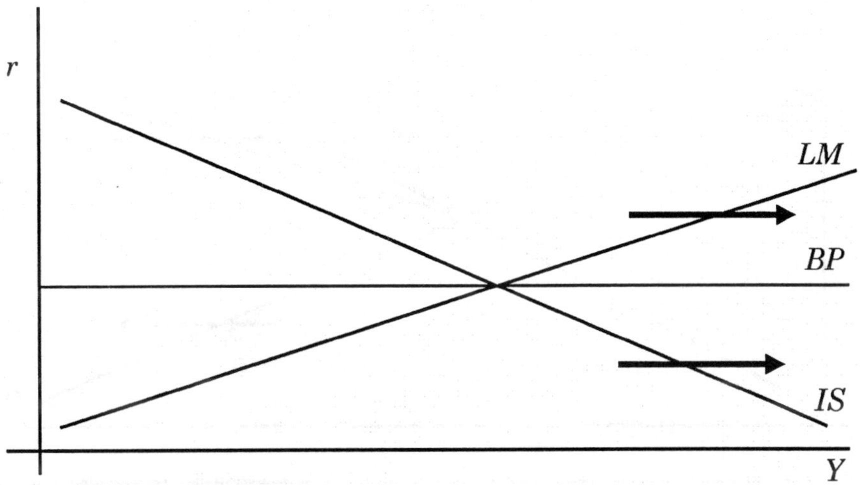

12.25 The mobility of international capital flows is:

(a) zero

(b) infinite

(c) less than infinite but not zero

(d) impossible to calculate from the information provided

12.26 The government decision is:

(a) tight monetary policy

(b) loose monetary policy

(c) tight fiscal policy

(d) loose fiscal policy

12.27 The exchange-rate régime is:

(a) floating

(b) fixed

(c) fixed with a devaluation

(d) impossible to assess from the information provided

Questions 12.28 to 12.33 refer to the economy that is described in the graph in Box 11. A government decision causes the shift in the LM line. The shift in the IS line and the shift in the BP line follow.

BOX 11

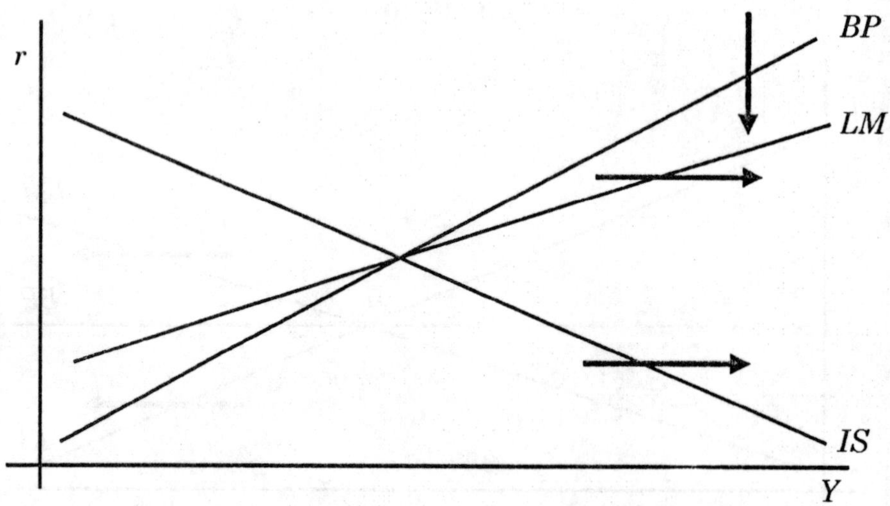

12.28 The mobility of international capital flows is:

(a) zero

(b) infinite

(c) less than infinite but greater than zero

(d) impossible to calculate from the information provided

12.29 The government decision is:

(a) tight monetary policy

(b) loose monetary policy

(c) tight fiscal policy

(d) loose fiscal policy

12.30 The exchange-rate régime is:

(a) floating

(b) fixed

(c) fixed with a devaluation

(d) impossible to assess from the information provided

12.31 The immediate effect, on the value of the local currency, of the government decision is:

(a) depreciation

(b) appreciation

(c) (a) or (b)

(d) neither (a) nor (b)

12.32 Following the immediate effect of the government decision, it is perceived that the value of the local currency is likely to:

(a) appreciate

(b) be stable

(c) depreciate

(d) (a) or (b) or (c)

12.33 The value of the elasticity of demand for net exports is:

(a) greater than one

(b) one

(c) less than one

(d) impossible to calculate from the information provided

12.34 The *BP* line usually slopes upward because the value of:

(a) net exports $[X - Z]$ is positively related to the level of income $[Y]$

(b) net international capital outflow $[F]$ is negatively related to the level of interest rates $[r]$

(c) (a) and (b)

(d) neither (a) nor (b)

12.35 If there is an increase in the level of interest rates in other countries (r_O), the *BP* line will:

(a) rotate clockwise

(b) rotate anti-clockwise

(c) shift parallel downwards

(d) shift parallel upwards

12.36 If there is an increase in the level of income in other countries (Yo), the *BP* line will:

(a) rotate clockwise

(b) rotate anti-clockwise

(c) shift parallel downwards

(d) shift parallel upwards

12.37 If there is an increase in the sensitivity of net international capital outflow (F) to changes in the local level of interest rates (r), the *BP* line will:

(a) rotate clockwise

(b) shift parallel downwards

(c) (a) and (b)

(d) neither (a) nor (b)

12.38 If there is an increase in the sensitivity of imports (Z) to changes in the level of income (Y), the *BP* line will:

(a) rotate clockwise

(b) shift parallel downwards

(c) (a) and (b)

(d) neither (a) nor (b)

Questions 12.39 to 12.41 refer to the economy whose international sector is described by the equations in Box 12.

BOX 12

Net outflow of capital (Rs. crore)	$F = 3 - 0.5r$
Exports (Rs. crore)	$X = 210$
Imports (Rs. crore)	$Z = 10 + 0.2Y$
Rate of interest (%)	$r = 5$
Income (Rs. crore)	$Y = 1000$

12.39 If there is a floating exchange rate policy, the effect on the value of the currency of the situation described is:

(a) an appreciation

(b) a depreciation

(c) neither (a) nor (b)

(d) impossible to calculate from the information provided

12.40 If there is a fixed exchange rate policy, and assuming that there is neither a devaluation nor a revaluation nor monetary sterilisation, the effect on the money supply (Ms) of the situation described is:

(a) an increase

(b) a decrease

(c) neither (a) nor (b)

(d) impossible to calculate from the information provided

12.41 The position of the *IS–LM* intersection is:

(a) above the *BP* line

(b) on the *BP* line

(c) below the *BP* line

(d) impossible to identify from the information provided

12.42 If the imports function shifts:

from $Z = 52 + 0.25Y$

to $Z = 67 + 0.38Y$

the *BP* line shifts to the:

(a) left and becomes steeper

(b) right and becomes steeper

(c) left and becomes less steep

(d) right and becomes less steep

12.43 If the net international capital outflow function shifts:

from $F = 12 - 148r$

to $F = 14 - 142r$

the shift of the *BP* line is:

(a) to the left and steeper

(b) to the right and steeper

(c) to the left and less steep

(d) impossible to identify from the information given

12.44 The *BP* line slopes downward:

(a) when the balance of trade is in deficit

(b) when the balance of payments is in deficit

(c) when the government budget balance is in deficit

(d) never

13

The Complete Model

No multiple-choice questions are listed for Chapters 13 and 14. Relevant questions are in *Thinking about Interest Rates, Prices, and the Economy* under earlier chapter headings. However, it is probably better, during the revision phase of a course, to encourage students to talk about, and to write about, the theory that has been studied.

This chapter is intended to remind students that, in macroeconomics, even simple models (such as the one in *Interest Rates, Prices, and the Economy*) are complex. Students should be able to discuss at length every part of Figure 82. They should understand, and be able to explain, the nature of each of four types of arrow and each of the four types of rectangle in this diagram. They should be able to explain the meaning of every arrow. These include the functional and arithmetic relationships in the diagram and also the feedback to each equilibrium process and constraint.

The purpose of economic models is to explain and predict changes in the values of variables, and students need to be able to distinguish the five types of processes that are included in Figure 82. Equilibrium processes determine the values of P, Y, and r (and also, if it is floating, the rate of exchange). Arithmetic definitions determine the values of the trade balance $[X - Z]$, the balance of payments $[X - Z - F]$, and the government budget balance $[T - G]$. There are also arithmetic aspects of the determination of the values of some of the other variables. In addition to the functional relationships shown, the variables on Figure 82 are subject to autonomous influences by changes in variables that are not shown. For example, the frequency of payments influences money demand $[M_D]$, the level of confidence influences planned expenditure $[E_P]$, political decisions influence government expenditure $[G]$, and economic and political conditions in other countries influence the value of exports $[X]$. Finally, political decisions determine the nature of the response to an unbalanced government budget, whether an exchange rate is fixed or floating, and whether a fixed exchange rate is devalued or revalued or neither.

A substantial amount of detail has been omitted from Figure 82 in order to fit the diagram on a single page of *Interest Rates, Prices, and the Economy*. Variables that do not appear on the diagram include C, I, S, M_D^T, M_D^P, and M_D^S.

The autonomous influences that are not shown in Figure 82 include the political dimensions of economic policy. For example, significant determinants of the macroeconomic outcome include whether the government principally targets a low inflation rate or a low unemployment rate, whether it prefers fiscal policy or monetary policy, whether it has promised tax cuts, whether it has promised low interest rates, whether it has promised an expansion of government-funded services, etc.

14

Conclusions: Overview of Macroeconomic Theory

This is a revision chapter. Relevant multiple-choice questions are under earlier chapter headings in *Thinking about Interest Rates, Prices, and the Economy*. Table 19 compares the key features of the macroeconomic models of Keynes and of the Classical economists. Table 20 compares the views of Keynesian and monetarist economists. It is important to be able to compare the assumptions and the conclusions of different theoretical approaches.

The intention both of Chapter 13 and of Chapter 14 is to encourage students to enhance their understanding of macroeconomic theory by reconsidering, in unfamiliar ways, material that has been learnt.

Glossary

Precise definitions are important partly because many of the technical words that are used in macroeconomic theory have different meanings in conversational usage. These include consumption, government spending, savings, income, injections, investment, and withdrawals. Even money has a meaning that many students do not anticipate.

Notation

Although advanced mathematics is not used in *Interest Rates, Prices, and the Economy*, simple algebra is used in most chapters. The notation needs to be fully understood. Any student who does not understand the meanings of the algebraic symbols will be unable to understand the theory that is presented in this book.

It is important to distinguish between stock variables (measured at a moment in time) and flow variables (measured over a period of time). For example, money demand [M_D] and money supply [M_S] are stock variables; demand for loanable funds [D_{LF}] and supply of loanable funds [S_{LF}] are flow variables.

Not all the macroeconomic variables that are explained in *Interest Rates, Prices, and the Economy* are measured in a money unit such as the Indian rupee. Another key distinction is between variables and parameters.

Answers

In this matrix of solutions to the multiple-choice questions in this book, columns identify chapter numbers and rows identify question numbers.

	0	1	2	3	4	5	6	7	8	9	10	11	12
1	c	d	b	b	c	d	c	c	c	c	d	b	a
2	a	b	b	d	c	c	d	a	a	c	d	a	d
3	d	d	a	b	a	c	a	c	d	b	a	b	b
4	c	a	b	a	a	b	d	c	c	d	c	a	d
5	b	c	c	a	a	d	a	a	d	d	c	c	c
6	b	c	c	a	c	a	c	a	d	a	b	c	a
7	c	d	a	a	d	c	a	c	d	d	c	a	d
8		a	b	b	a	c	a	a	c	a	b	d	b
9			c	c	d	c	a	a	b	b	d	c	a
10			a	b	d	a	d	b	d	a		c	c
11			a	d	b	a	a		b	c		d	a
12			a	b	d	d	b		c	d		b	d
13			c	a	c	a	a		c	a		c	b

	0	1	2	3	4	5	6	7	8	9	10	11	12
14			d	c	a	d	a		b	b		c	a
15			b	a	d	c	d		c	a		b	b
16			c	d	d	d	b		b	a		d	b
17			b	c	c	a	c		d	d		b	a
18			a	c	c	c	a		b	d		c	d
19			c	c	c	b	d					c	d
20			b	d	d	b	b					c	c
21			b		d	c	d					c	a
22			a		c	c	b					a	b
23			b		b	c	c					d	b
24			d		b	d	b					c	d
25			a		d	a	c					b	b
26			c		b	a	b					c	b
27			a		d	b	c					a	a
28			a			a	a					d	c
29			a			c	b					d	b
30			b			d	d					c	a
31			b				c					b	a
32			d				a						a
33			d				c						a
34			d				b						b
35			d				a						d

	0	1	2	3	4	5	6	7	8	9	10	11	12
36			d				d						c
37			c				c						c
38			c				b						d
39			d				a						b
40			d				c						b
41			a				a						c
42			c				d						a
43			a				c						a
44			c				b						d
45							c						
46							d						
47							a						
48							c						
49							b						